The Million Dollar Voicem☎il Practices *Handbook*

The Million Dollar Voicemail Practices Handbook

Robert Grant

Bravery of Muskrats

Portland, Ore.

Published by Bravery of Muskrats, Portland, Ore.

ISBN: 978-0-578-57650-3

Dedicated to Keith, Paula, & Shannon
for your incredible generosity,
mentorship, and encouragement

Contents

Calls That Go to Voicemail

Calls that go to voicemail go to the next business that answers their phone.

People Are Busy

Jane is a high-powered attorney.

Jane is also her ailing mother's closest living relative, which means it is Jane who takes care of her mother's finances, takes her to get her hair done, and goes along on all of her doctor appointments.

Her mother long ago stopped driving, but for reasons of both nostalgia and practicality, she refused to sell her car. It was the only car she and her late husband ever bought new. It was the car they took on their first cross-country road trip (the first time she'd ever left the state!). It was the car they drove their grandchildren around in.

She liked the memories it contained.

As for practicality, she didn't think it would be fair to Jane to put "all that wear and tear" on Jane's vehicle, so whenever Jane picked her up, she insisted they drive the Pontiac—and that she be allowed to pay for the gas.

This past weekend, while taking her mother out shopping, Jane heard an awful clunking sound while making left turns. She made herself a note to call a repair shop first thing Monday morning.

By the time "first thing" Monday morning rolled around, Jane had already been at the office for two hours working on a case. She had ten minutes before she had to attend her Monday morning partners meeting, so she paused to schedule the appointment to have her mom's car fixed.

Not having a preferred mechanic, she went online and Googled "auto repair" for her local area. She called the first reputable-looking business.

The call went to voicemail.

Her thought process: "If I leave a message, they'll probably call back while I'm in my meeting…and by the time I'm able to call *them* back, who knows, they may be busy or on their lunch break. I don't have time to play phone tag today. I need to get this done and off my plate."

And faster than you can say *"lost initial sale, lost follow-up sale, and lost referral sale,"* Jane hung up the phone and called the next reputable-looking business on the list.

People Procrastinate

A few years ago, my wife and I got behind on our yard work, which is to say *I* got behind on our yard work. Big time.

By the time I finally took care of all the mowing, trimming, pruning, and uprooting that was needed to get back into the good graces of our neighbors, I had filled a dozen heavy-duty lawn and leaf bags. And the debris that I couldn't put in the bags (like dirt and branches) resembled a poorly-made beaver dam behind our garage.

A week passed and I still hadn't made arrangements to have the bags and debris hauled away. Then another week passed. Then another.

My wife politely asked when that might be happening. "Soon," I said, "very soon."

Two weeks later, "soon" had not yet come to pass.

Our next conversation was more explicit: "I would like that junk removed before I'm in the back yard gardening this weekend," she said. "It needs to go." I said I'd take care of it within the week.

I wish I could tell you that it was an uncharacteristically busy start to the week, with several unexpected "fires" demanding my urgent attention. But it wasn't. And there weren't. For whatever reason, I simply had a mental block about calling to schedule that junk removal.

By Thursday morning, I was in a panic: "I'm in serious trouble if I don't get that handled by tomorrow afternoon!"

Before I went on my lunch break, I Googled "junk removal" and wrote down the names and numbers of the three most professional-looking businesses. Then I grabbed some drive-thru food and scarfed it down in the parking lot before calling the first business on my list.

That call went to voicemail.

Faster than you can say *"lost initial sale, lost follow-up sale, and lost referral sale,"* I hung up the phone and called the next business. They answered the phone and got the job.

Let's face it: people procrastinate. Office managers procrastinate on their paper supply orders. Restaurant managers procrastinate on their food supply orders. Travelers procrastinate on their hotel and rental car bookings. Golfers procrastinate on their tee times. Homeowners procrastinate on all sorts of things: calling the plumber, calling the roofer, calling the electrician, calling the handyman. And so on.

People procrastinate.

Often times, by the time people finally get around to calling a business for help, they need help *now*. As such, they have no time for voicemail. They simply call the next business on the list.

People Have Options

Few businesses have the luxury of being the only one of their kind in town. To gain initial, follow-up, and referral sales, businesses need to seize any possible opportunity to provide better service than the competition. Answering the phone (instead of letting calls go to voicemail) is one way to do that.

When it comes down to it, people don't need or want *you*, they need or want the products and services you provide— and options abound.

Don't Confuse a Nibble
for a Hooked Fish

That said, sometimes callers do leave voicemails.

But don't confuse a nibble on your line for a hooked fish. That same caller who left you a voicemail at 7:36am might have left a voicemail for one of your competitors at 7:39am.

In those instances, the first business that calls the customer back wins.

The First Thing You Do

In light of the previous chapter, I suggest that

❏ Check Voicemail

be the first thing you do:

- as soon as you get to work
- as soon as you get back from a coffee break
- as soon as you get back from a bathroom break
- as soon as you get back from a lunch break
- as soon as you get back from running
  to the post office, etc.

Anytime you're away from your desk for more than thirty seconds—or whenever you are aware that you've missed a call because you were on the other line or providing face-to-face help to a customer—the first thing you should do when you return is check your voicemail.[1] And then you should immediately return any calls.

---

[1] *This should also be one of the last things you do before leaving for the day.*

The Second Thing You Do

I've mentioned that people are busy and that they procrastinate.

People are also impulsive and fickle, which is why I suggest that

❑ Check Caller ID

be the second thing you do:

- as soon as you get to work
- as soon as you get back from a coffee break
- as soon as you get back from a bathroom break
- as soon as you get back from a lunch break
- as soon as you get back from running
  to the post office, etc.

Consider the following scenario:

Steven's car is eight years old. He has owned it for six of those eight years and a majority of its 103,281 miles. He's ready for a change.

For going on two years now, Steven has been completely enamored with a certain make and model of car. A regular diet of national TV ads, along with local radio ads and billboards—as well as the dozens of eye-catching "testimonials" he sees on the road everyday—has finally moved him to action. Late one Saturday morning, he calls the local dealership to see if they have any fully-loaded, silver sedans in stock that he could test drive.

The phone rings…and rings…and rings…and rings…and goes to voicemail.

Rather than leave a message, Steven decides he'll just "try them again in a few minutes."

A few minutes later, however, Steven is kicked back in his recliner, fully engrossed in a college football shootout between two of the nation's top-ranked teams. Ten minutes go by. Then thirty minutes. Then an hour. Calling the dealership back has slipped his mind.

He might have remembered to call the dealership once the game was over, but just as the fourth quarter is drawing to a close, a buddy calls to see if Steven wants to grab some wings and catch the late matinee of the new Bond movie. "See you in twenty minutes!"

As Steven is driving to the restaurant, he talks himself into hanging onto his current car for a couple more years.

. . .

Anytime you're away from your desk for more than thirty seconds (or whenever you are aware that you've missed a call because you were on the other line or providing face-to-face help to a customer), the second thing you should do when you return is check Caller ID.[2] And then you should immediately return any calls.

Had an enthusiastic, confident, sales-minded receptionist done that with Steven's missed call, that dealership may well have made a sale that day—even if Steven had initially objected to the receptionist's invitation to come in:

> STEVEN
> (relaxed in his recliner)
> Oh, I'm all settled in watching the Florida-LSU game now. Maybe I'll stop in later today when the game's over and after I've run a few errands. How late are you open?

> RECEPTIONIST
> How much time is left in the game?

> STEVEN
> (surprised by her question)
> Um… It's just the start of the second quarter…so—

> RECEPTIONIST
> (playfully interrupting)
> Pft! That game is barely getting started. You could come on down, test drive a couple different models, and still catch the fourth quarter, which, if it's like most games, is the only quarter you really need to catch. You could even watch the rest of the game here in our customer service lounge over a free bag of popcorn. How soon could you be here?

You get the idea.

Depending on your call volume, systematically checking for and immediately responding to missed calls [that do not leave a message but can be retrieved by checking Caller ID] could easily result in one additional sales opportunity each week for your business. Perhaps more. Perhaps many more.

There's a great deal of truth in this statement by David Noonan: "In the end, it is attention to detail that makes all the difference. It's the center fielder's extra two steps to the left, the sales[person]'s memory for names, the lover's phone call, the soldier's clean weapon. It is the thing that separates the winners from the losers, the men [and women] from the boys [and girls], and, very often, the living from the dead."

Attention (or inattention) to detail can set your business on a path to unprecedented success (or lost sales).

[2]*This should also be one of the last things you do before leaving for the day.*

The Caller's Perception

Upon pulling an "Inbound Calls" report for a company I was doing some consulting work for recently, here's what I saw:

Day	Hour	Source	Duration	Caller #
Wed	7:16am	Newspr	0:01:17	xxx-xxx-2279
Wed	7:34am	Newspr	0:00:57	xxx-xxx-5541
Wed	7:42am	DirMail	0:01:25	xxx-xxx-1345
Wed	7:53am	Newspr	0:00:32	xxx-xxx-9835
Wed	7:59am	Newspr	0:01:04	xxx-xxx-3178
Wed	8:37am	Newspr	0:00:34	xxx-xxx-5081
Wed	8:46am	DirMail	0:07:29	xxx-xxx-8717
Wed	9:18am	Newspr	0:00:14	xxx-xxx-5081
Wed	9:22am	Newspr	0:00:13	xxx-xxx-5081
Wed	10:03am	DirMail	0:03:38	xxx-xxx-7651
Wed	10:19am	Newspr	0:11:46	xxx-xxx-0825
Wed	11:38am	Internet	0:04:42	xxx-xxx-9420
Wed	11:51am	Newspr	0:05:26	xxx-xxx-1380
Wed	12:05pm	DirMail	0:00:19	xxx-xxx-3728

There are a couple things that really jumped out at me.

First off, the regular business hours for this company were 9am to 5:30pm, with the receptionist typically arriving for work between 8:40am and 8:45am. That means the first six calls of the day went straight to voicemail. Not good.

(My recommendation: On days when they know their newspaper ad will be hitting homes, make sure someone is staffing their telephones between 7am and 8:45am, at least until such a time as they notice a decrease in this level of early-morning call volume.)

The other thing that really jumped out at me was the three missed calls from the caller whose number ends in 5081. All three calls went straight to voicemail—and in all three instances the caller hung up without leaving a message.

At 8:37am the receptionist wasn't at work yet to answer the phone. At 9:18am she may have been on the other line and unable to graciously hang up on the person she was speaking with (or even put them on hold) to grab the incoming call. At 9:22am she may have noticed, through the window in the waiting area, that a man crossing the parking lot had dropped a glove and gone out to retrieve it for him.

In short, she may well have been attentively and conscientiously doing her job when those calls at 9:18am and 9:22am went straight to voicemail.

But to the caller whose number ends in 5081, the *perception* was that the receptionist *wasn't* doing her job. The caller's perception was that their calls—and their business—weren't important to this company.

In rare instances, people who feel they've received sub-par customer service will call the manager to complain. More often, however, they'll simply call the next business on the list,[3] which I suspect was the case with this caller, as there was no record of them calling back the rest of the day.

Because the receptionist was not in the practice of checking Caller ID,[4] a prospective sale, follow-up sale, and referral sale were lost.

[3] *When it comes down to it, customers don't need or want you, they need or want the products and services you provide—and options abound.*

[4] *To be fair—and perhaps more to the point—the receptionist's manager was not in the practice of encouraging and requiring her to check Caller ID.*

What to Say

When you return a missed call, here's a simple, straightforward way to engage the customer:

> "Hi, this is Carla with the Rest Well Motor Lodge.
> I see we missed a call from you a few minutes
> ago. How may we help you today?"

Here's another example, with slight variation:

> "Hi, this is Rick with Eastside Realty. I see we
> missed a call from you this morning. How can we
> help you today?"

Simply substitute your name, your company's name, and the time the call was missed. Hopefully you'll be responding to missed calls so quickly that you'll always be saying "a few minutes ago" instead of the more general "this morning" or "this afternoon."

One front desk associate I worked with had a concern that people would be "weirded out" and find it a little creepy that the business she worked for was calling people back who didn't leave a message. Twenty years ago that might have been the case, but these days practically everyone has Caller ID and accepts it as a normative part of our phone culture.

In my experience, I've never once heard of someone bristling or expressing indignation that they were being called back after a missed call. In fact, the opposite is often true. In a world where actual messages can go unresponded to for hours (if not days), I've found that promptly returning a missed call often catches people off guard in a *"Wow, talk about responsive customer service!"* kind of way.

People delight in having their expectations exceeded.

The Fourth
(HUGE) Benefit

So far, we've touched on three benefits to regularly checking your voicemail and Caller ID—and immediately returning any calls:

1) you will be responding to customers before your competition does,
2) you will be promptly re-engaging ready-to-buy customers who hang up without leaving a message, and
3) you will be exceeding customers' expectations by promptly returning their missed calls.

There's a fourth benefit, and it's HUGE. It has to do with managing—and maximizing—your appointment calendar.

In the industry I most recently came from full-time, the hearing aid industry, it wasn't uncommon for people to cancel their appointment the day of, for a variety of reasons: illness, transportation, scheduling conflict, etc. Days that looked promising the evening before (from a sales-opportunity standpoint) could quickly turn into an exercise in thumb-twiddling futility. Not good for sales—or morale. (And things that aren't good for morale can be devastating for sales.)

There was also a correlation between "lead time" and "show rate." By lead time, I mean the number of days between when a customer called in and when their appointment was scheduled for. The longer the lead time, the less likely the customer was to show for their appointment.

Here's how all of this relates to checking voicemail and Caller ID:

Scenario #1:
Shelly is the receptionist for Choose Better Hearing. It's 8:50am on a Wednesday morning, and their schedule for that day and the rest is the week is packed. The first customer is scheduled to arrive in ten minutes and Shelly still has to turn on the lights, turn on the computers, turn on the DVD loop in the waiting area, make coffee, unlock the doors, check voicemail, and run to the restroom. She's feeling rushed.

As luck would have it, the 9am customer, Mr. Williams, shows up early. A little flustered, Shelly unlocks the doors, turns on the lights, and excuses herself to go use the restroom. When she returns, she hands Mr. Williams and his wife an intake form to fill out and she politely asks if they would like any coffee. "That'd be great," they say.

Shelly disappears into the back room to make coffee. No sooner does she push "Brew" and the phone rings. It's a customer calling in off that morning's newspaper ad, wanting to come in for a free hearing test.

Shelly turns on her computer and logs into the appointment calendar. "Okay... It looks like our first available appointment is next Monday morning.

Or we have an opening on Tuesday afternoon. Would either of those work for you?" The caller, Susan Baker, sounds disappointed that she has to wait until next week to get in, but she agrees to the Monday morning appointment. Shelly gathers the relevant contact information and schedules the appointment. "Great," says Shelly, wrapping up the call, "we'll see you next Monday!"

Fifteen minutes later, after the hearing instrument specialist has invited Mr. Williams and his wife back into the testing room and Shelly has turned on the DVD loop, she finally gets around to checking voicemail. The first message is from a telemarketer. The second message is from Mrs. Smith calling to cancel her husband's appointment for later that afternoon because he's come down with the flu. Mrs. Smith says she'll call to reschedule when he's feeling better.

Shelly isn't present to this reality, but her decision to not prioritize checking voicemail and Caller ID just cost Choose Better Hearing $12,000 in lost sales over the next four years.

The very next day, Ms. Baker sees a competitor's ad in the paper, running a sale that appears comparable to the sale Choose Better Hearing ran the day before. Ms. Baker calls the number in the ad. Lo and behold they have an opening that afternoon and would be happy to test her hearing. By 4:30pm, Ms. Baker is driving home wearing a pair of open-fit hearing aids, and for the first time in seven years, she can hear the flutes in Mozart's Symphony No. 39.

Three years later, she upgrades to a pair of blue-tooth-enabled hearing aids. And a year after that, she finally convinces her brother Bill to buy a pair.

Just like that: $12,000 in lost sales.

Scenario #2:
Same as above, except that instead of seeing and calling the competitor's ad the next day, Ms. Baker sees an ad for an 11-day cruise "exploring Anchorage and Denali National Park"—a lifelong dream of hers that she's put off and put off.

No longer! On a wave of whimsy, she calls and books a reservation for her and her daughter.

The following Monday, Ms. Baker comes to the conclusion that, in light of the Alaskan cruise, she's going to have to put her hearing aid purchase on hold for awhile. She calls and cancels her appointment.

Had Shelly prioritized checking voicemail and Caller ID on Wednesday morning, she'd have known about Mr. Smith's cancelled appointment *before* Ms. Baker called about getting her hearing tested…and instead of booking an Alaskan cruise, Ms. Baker would be booking a reservation for her and her daughter to attend a performance of their local symphony!

If either of these scenarios plays out even just once a month, that is potentially setting in motion $144,000 in lost sales over a four-year period. And if that is happening year after year after year—as it is for many businesses—over a nine- or ten-year period, you're looking at $1 million in lost sales,[5] perhaps more depending on what a typical sale (or typical customer) is worth to you and how many businesses/locations you own or manage.

---

[5] *And that's just the lost sales. This figure doesn't take into account the lost technology upgrades, the lost training events, the lost advertising initiatives, the lost employee-retaining bonuses, etc., which are the unfortunate and very real by-products of lost sales—which, in turn, perpetuate lost sales.*

Your Outgoing
Voicemail Message

In the unfortunate event that a customer's call should go to voicemail (rather than be answered by your enthusiastic, confident, sales-minded receptionist), it is important that your outgoing voicemail message elicits the desired response: an inbound voicemail message complete with the caller's name and number.

To that end, I suggest you keep your outgoing message brief (thirty seconds or less) and that it contains the following five elements, in this order:

- Gratitude
- Value (relationship, NOT selling)
- Information
- Call to action
- Value (relationship, NOT selling)

Here is an example:

"Thank you for calling Vision by Mike, where we help people with vision loss see clearly again! If you are receiving this message during regular business hours, we are currently helping a customer. Our regular hours are Monday through Friday from 10am to 6pm, with evenings and weekends available by special appointment. Please leave a name and number and we will return your call as soon as we receive your message. We look forward to helping you see better!"

Here's another example:

> "Thank you for calling River Ridge Hardware, your one-stop source for hardware supplies and helpful, expert advice. If you are receiving this message during our regular business hours of Monday through Saturday, from 7am to 6pm, we are currently helping a customer. Please leave a name and number and we will return your call as soon as we receive your message. We look forward to helping you with your project!"

If River Ridge Hardware was going to be closed for, say, the 4th of July, they'd want to update their voicemail message before leaving work the night before:

> "Thank you for calling River Ridge Hardware, your one-stop source for hardware supplies and helpful, expert advice. We will be closed on the 4th of July to give our employees the chance to celebrate with their families. We will resume our regular business hours of Monday through Saturday, from 7am to 6pm, beginning on the 5th. Feel free to leave a name and number and we will return your call as soon as we receive your message. We look forward to helping you with your project!"

Scripting your message is half the battle. The other half is recording it.

It is important that you choose "the voice of your company" carefully, making sure of all the following:

- man or woman with a strong, clear voice
- NOT the voice of an employee who no longer works for you
- voice has an engaging quality that draws you in and compels you to keep listening:
  - every word is distinctly and carefully pronounced
  - good pacing (not so rushed that words bleed together, but neither so slow that people who are highly time-sensitive start to get anxious)
  - warm and natural-sounding (as opposed to emotionally dry and overly clinical- or commercial-sounding)

It's also important that the recording be done in a quiet place, free from any background noise that might distract— or worse, dissuade—the caller.

The sooner your outgoing voicemail message meets the above criteria, the better.

P.S.　You may have noticed that I left out the phrase "your call is very important to us." That was intentional. Whenever I hear "your call is very important to us" on a pre-recorded voicemail message, the little voice in my head *always* says, "Really? If my call is so important to you, then why didn't you answer your phone!?" That phrase is an immediate trigger for annoyance and frustration. (Surely, I am not alone in this.) That is why I left out that phrase and suggest you do the same.

P.P.S.　There is more than one way to craft an effective voicemail message. If you find the above formula helpful, great. If not, no problem. Feel free to experiment.

Again, what's important is that your outgoing message be brief, engaging, and that it elicits the desired response: an inbound voicemail message complete with the caller's name and number.

Something to Consider

You spend a lot of money to make the phone ring. And those folks calling you aren't just anybody—they're the lifeblood of your company or organization.

You can't survive without them.

Hopefully, this concise handbook has helped give you a greater appreciation for just how important it is to be intentional and systematic in your approach to voicemail.

In addition to

- recording a brief, engaging outgoing voicemail message,
- regularly checking your voicemail and Caller ID, and
- immediately responding to any voicemails or missed calls,

you may want to implement some call tracking software.[6] I've used call tracking software extensively and have found it to be an invaluable tool.

Not only does call tracking help ensure that "missed" calls are no longer missed, it also allows you to see exactly which ads are making the phone ring, when those calls are coming in, how many calls get answered, how long those calls last, how many calls go to voicemail, how many callers hang up before going to voicemail, etc.

Again, attention (or inattention) to detail can set your business on a path to unprecedented success (or lost sales).

Something to consider.

[6]*The various call tracking software I have experience with has been packaged with call recording/playback features. Be sure to check your state and federal laws before using such features.*

About the Author

Robert Grant is co-founder of Essendio Consulting & Creative, whose mission is to help businesses, organizations, and individuals make their work more enjoyable and more profitable.

More information at:
www.essendioconsulting.com

Notes

Notes